POETRY &
PRAYER

by
Kathryn Boyd

POETRY &
PRAYER

by Kathryn Boyd

Southern
Arizona
Press

Southern Arizona Press
Sierra Vista, Arizona

Poetry & Prayer

By Kathryn Boyd

First Edition

Author: Kathryn Boyd
Editor: Paul Gilliland
Formatting: Southern Arizona Press
Cover Photograph: Madison Boyd
Cover Design: Paul Gilliland

Published by Southern Arizona Press
Sierra Vista, Arizona 85635
www.SouthernArizonaPress.com

ISBN: 978-1-960038-40-1

Poetry

DEDICATION

To Deacon Chris Anderson

Thank you for reminding me that the voice of doubt is never the voice of God, for teaching me that my writing is my way of reaching out to God and of God reaching out to me, and for helping me believe that poetry is a form of prayer.

CONTENTS

MY GARDEN

In the garden of my mind
My inner critic weeds
Raking away the positive
In its place, planting negative seeds
Hoping it can grow
A patch of bitterness
Bearing fruits of anger
Resentment and wickedness
The ivy may be poison
Just like my critic's thoughts
Choking out the fresh new growth
Until everything begins to rot
Little does my critic know
That I'm a gardener too
And where the soil has been plowed
New crops begin anew
I water them with prayers
Until the roots grab hold
Producing a harvest in my mind
Of a garden that blooms gold

TORNADO

There are some days that I feel weak
Yet others where I feel strong
Then there are times that whatever I do
It seems to be all wrong
It's like I've buckled myself in
Preparing for the crash
Not knowing what may be ahead
In my day-to-day forecast
Sometimes I feel as if
It's just me against the world
As if everyone else's frustration
Combines with mine to hurl
Like a tornado violently destroying
Everything that lays in its path
Leaving broken pieces
To be collected in the aftermath
Sometimes I am going nowhere
Yet everywhere at the same time
My thoughts are running in circles
The worn-out face in the mirror is mine
I bleed when I fall down
Holding the weight of the world on my shoulders
Please accept my apology
If occasionally I lose my composure

FALLEN FAITH

My faith is sometimes shaken
And I question my beliefs
I feel as if I'm all alone
As negativity defeats
I forget to kneel upon the ground
With head bowed down in prayer
Instead, I battle on my own
Losing the war to despair
My hopes lay scattered at my feet
Rather than bundled up in faith
There they end up trampled on
Instead of in God's embrace
I need to make the choice to trust
Even in uncertain times
Stop from walking the path of fear
Stay open to God's many signs

INTERNAL CONFLICT

Internal conflict
The going over and over something
A million plus times in your head
Sleepless nights
Constant anxiety
Playing out a variety of scenarios
Overthinking until you can't think anymore
Even harder than the decision
Is thinking about the result of what you've decided
Life isn't black or white
Obsessing over whether your choice is right or wrong
Will you be rewarded or punished?
Decisions are a series of possibilities
Of hope
Of growth
Reflection
Picking a new path
Trusting your own intuition

DIFFERENCES

Why does it seem that everyone
Sees only in black or white?
Where they believe their opinions
Are the only ones that are right?
What is so difficult about
Trying on someone else's shoes?
Maybe try to look at things
From another's point of view?
Everyday people quarrel
Carrying heaviness by their side
With a difference of opinions
Creating a huge divide
Why can't it be remembered
We all journey across this land?
Scattered with an array of colors
Meant to help us understand
That the paths we choose aren't easy
But the choices are ours to make
It shouldn't be anyone else's business
On how our future takes its shape
When you look out at your neighbor
Remember, their life reads different than yours
We celebrate our own triumphs
We fight individual wars

GHOST

Please don't sketch me in pencil
Or scratch me out with pen
Don't erase me from this life
Or black out my written name
I have become a ghost to some
Faded away to many others
A whisper of a memory
That's never fully recovered
My footsteps fall invisibly
I have a voice that carries no sound
The person I once was
Is nowhere to be found
I ask that you open up your eyes
Let your senses begin to roam free
Maybe you'll feel the shimmering touch
Of the ghost that I call me

EMPTY SPACES

If you find your heart has holes
Where empty spaces dwell
Don't panic and think you're incomplete
Or that your heart is just a shell
Sometimes those empty spaces
Are really meant to be
They allow for new experiences
For old hurt to be set free
That hurt may be a person
Who your heart needs to let go
For if that person were to remain
A weedy thorn may grow
That weed would start to feel wrong
As it grows out of control
Infecting all within its reach
'Til your heart begins to decompose
Please don't fret those empty spaces
Or ever think they're wrong
For now, there's room for light to shine
On the things that make you strong

CRUMBLING

I don't want you to see me crumble
As this autoimmune disease takes its hold
My bones are undeniably tired
With pain that travels but never shows
I try to hide the heat of fire
That constantly burns inside
It steals my day and sometimes my night
With lonely pain and silent cries
I keep on going; must not stop
Can't spent my life in bed
Can't process words with this foggy brain
Leaving so many thoughts unsaid
I dream of escaping this endless cycle
As my muscles restrict every move
Your hug should be that caring touch
Not something that feels cruel
There are days the base of my skull
Seems to be sitting on a spike
Causing energy and fatigue
To clash and pick a fight
Leaving me battling anxiety
Where depression always wins
But to keep you from witnessing me crumble
I hide it all behind a fake grin

MY OUTDOOR CHURCH

I don't need a church pew
Every Sunday morning
Not because I don't believe
Or I find the homily boring
All I need is to step outside
To take a look around
Try to quiet my buzzing thoughts
Walk barefoot on the ground
Feel the breeze that cools my skin
From the warmth the sun provides
Set my gaze upon the view
Where mountains meet the sky
Listen to the song of birds
Catch the scent of blooming flowers
Watch the continuous changing clouds
With every passing hour
As I watch the setting sun
I thank the Lord above
For His never-ending presence
And His unconditional love

MY MUSE

I wonder where my muse has gone
And why she disappeared
I wonder what has her upset
Are my thoughts what she has feared?
All I know is my pen has stopped
Scratching across the paper
Leaving words lodged in my mind
Accusing my muse of a traitor
She's probably off on vacation
Building castles in the sand
Stretched out beside the crashing waves
Skin golden with suntan
Maybe she's deep in a forest
That's surrounded in mystique
Lost within its solitude
Toes dangling in a creek
She's left me feeling lost and alone
No inspiration to describe such tragedy
Wherever my muse may be hiding
She is safe from my insanity

SINCE I'M ONLY HUMAN

Since I'm only human
I tend to make mistakes
Apologies roll off my tongue
I often fall from grace
I learn from every stumble
Each mountain that I climb
Staying focused on the heavens
Seeking strength from the divine
But being human can sometimes hurt
When the heavens lose their focus
Leaving thoughts tied up in tangled knots
A broken heart and hopeless
It's me against the world
In a fight I can't seem to win
Someday I will face my final judgment
I will pay for my every sin
But when I get to heaven
I hope that He forgives
Remembering I was only human
Absolving the wrong that I did

THE POWER OF A WORD

Beware of words that come from your mouth
Watch out for the tone they may carry
Are they argumentative, sarcastic, vindictive?
Leaving those who receive them a bit weary?
Be careful of judgment and criticism
Without first examining yourself
A constant attack on others
May leave them waving farewell
Be cautious of the words "I would never"
For someday you just might
Then you will eat crow for dinner
Choking on every bite
Wash down the negativity
With a glass of something half full
Speak kind words of encouragement
Until positivity is habitual

HOURGLASS

Soon to be lost forever
Time is moving far too fast
It slips straight through my hands
Like grains of sand in an hourglass
I never told you what
It is I should've said
I just held it in
Locked in my heart instead
I was scared of all the things I've done
Afraid you wouldn't understand
Even though I'm not the only one
Whose apologies are in demand
The day will come to face it all
When I must stand my ground
There you may find me lost and lonely
Or even broken down
The devil's been whispering in my ear
Leaving me uneasy in my skin
When the earth crumbles under my feet
Pray it buries all my sin
I wish I could hit rewind
Instead of hanging by a thread
Doubting all that I believed
Regretting words I left unsaid

MIDNIGHT'S BATTLE

As the world is deeply sleeping
The hours ticking slowly by
You lay with your eyes open
Frustrated and wondering why
May it be you're afraid of sleep
And the nightmares it may bring?
Counting mistakes instead of sheep
Letting the painful memories sting
You tuck them back into your soul
At the dawning of morning's light
Where they stay until the midnight hour
In preparation for another fight

DEAR CHARLIE

Why did you have to go
And leave me here alone?
Wondering what I could have said
If only I had known
You must've been drowning in darkness
Unable to feel the light
Was there anything I could've done
To keep you safe that night?
Were you dancing with your demons?
Or dangling from a cliff?
Were storm clouds gathering overhead
As you felt your world begin to shift?
I cannot untangle the thoughts
That continue to ravage my mind
The torment that I feel
Knowing I was completely blind
Your story ended way too soon
No one but God knows why
All I know is my life's been changed
I never got to say goodbye

In memory of Charles O'Brien
10/29/1982 - 09/02/2020

TOO YOUNG

I wish I could communicate
With those who've gone before
Tell them how I miss them
Ask what's behind my future's door
Have those conversations
I didn't have when they were here
Because I didn't stop to consider
That one day they'd disappear
Listen to the wisdom
That they surely have to share
Since they've traveled through both worlds
They could help me to prepare
For struggles in my future
Heartache yet to come
The process of forgiveness
My destiny's outcome
I wish I'd taken time
To learn their fears and dreams
What it was that made them tick
And everything in between
For as you journey through this life
And all is said and done
No matter how long you're on this earth
Everyone dies too young

MY LIFE IS LIKE A PIECE OF PAPER

My life is like a piece of paper
Words written
Scratched out
Erased
At times it's brittle and thin
The edges ragged and torn
It's all a story
Each mark a piece of history
What gets written
Can never be used again
Others can read the words
But not all understand their meaning
Light it on fire and it will burn
Hold on too tight and it will crumple
Too loosely and it will blow away
Held up to the sun
Light shines through
Blank lines are waiting
For my story to continue
No two chapters are the same
My life is like a piece of paper
Sometimes it's bound tight and sturdy
At others, it's brittle and thin

INVISIBLE PAIN

I'm sorry if my actions
May sometimes seem wrong
It's my hope that you can understand
Why there are times I am withdrawn
I miss out on opportunities
As they pass throughout my day
I find that my mind and body
Tend to disobey
I find I get discouraged
When once again fatigued
Yet finding myself exhausted
Doesn't mean sleep is guaranteed
You may think I am not listening
When I hear every word you say
Information doesn't process quickly
My response a bit delayed
I work on wearing a smile
But sometimes the tears just fall
It's not always due to sadness
It's when invisible pain assaults
Please don't be quick to judge
Or point out what you think is wrong
You may not understand
But to this pain I belong

SOMEONE

Someone knows your secrets
Someone knows your name
Someone knows down deep inside
You take on all the blame
Someone knows you're hurting
Hiding all that pain
Only letting tears flow
When they can blend in with the rain
Someone knows your faults
Someone knows your fears
Someone sees quite clearly
Things aren't always as they appear
Someone's always with you
Offering a love that should be known
For it's a love like no other
With Him you're never alone

PURPOSE

Have you ever looked for answers
In places unknown?
Been in a crowded room
Yet completely alone?
We all feel numb
At one time or another
We want our buried feelings
To be rediscovered
Go ahead and tell me
What is it you want to say?
I will sit here and listen
Save you from losing your way
We all need connections
A way to keep holding on
To keep our head above water
As the world spins dusk to dawn
For have you ever felt
Like you've breathed your last breath?
Wonder if you're drowning
In the tears that you've wept?
We all feel at times
As if the steps we take are wrong
As if there is nowhere
We really belong
But this journey has purpose
Do the best that you can
No matter the where or when
I will be there offering my hand

THE GIRL I CALL ME

Some say you will understand
Once you get older
I must still be a kid
'Cause I'm still searching for closure
I want my space
Yet I want to fit in
Wishing things would end
So I could begin again
I am a little worn out
Not completely broken down
Wishing the words from my mouth
Sounded a bit more profound
I just need a moment to breathe
'Cause my edges are rough
Even with life's scratches and scars
Things can be patched up
I have a picture in my head
Of what I could turn out to be
If I just took a little more time
To understand the girl I call me

SEEDLING

Come, sit, and listen
There's a story the wind holds
An inkling of truth
Hidden behind lies big and bold
Whispered from mouths
Of friend and foe
Not bothering to care
How gossip does grow
It's a little seed planted
Then watered and fed
Until the speck of truth
Becomes buried and dead
Taking along with it
To its grave
A person's right to privacy
Thanks to those who misbehave

Kathryn Boyd

BOTTLED UP

I will not say I'm sorry
For the tears that I shed
Don't you dare start saying
That it's all in my head
My emotions are real
Slightly out of control
Spiraling quickly
Towards the black hole
It's built-up anger, fear and pain
Don't pity me now
For I am to blame
I bottle my feelings
Until the pressure's too much
The tears gush free
At the tiniest touch

LOST

Everyone carries a brokenness
That hides inside ourselves
It sits beside our memories
And in our soul it dwells
This world can leave us feeling
Like we've lost who we once were
We catch a glimpse within our shadow
Desire begins to stir
A longing for what used to be
Things that might have been
We find that we start praying
For healing to begin
No one likes to feel lost
In knowing who they are
We need to keep pushing onward
Keep our gaze upon the stars
With our focus on the sun and moon
Our heart might find content
If our brokenness can reach that place
Our life has been well spent

SELF-PITY ROAD

You set off down the road
Towards a place that most deplore
Lost within your private thoughts
Arriving at self-pity's door
You forgot to offer up a smile
To that stranger on the street
Neglect to finish minor tasks
Leaving them incomplete
Stumbling around amidst the dark
Not allowing any light to shine
Swallows up your positive energy
Relationships steadily decline
You find yourself lost without a map
Too many mistakes to amend
Blocking your mind to your surroundings
Leaves you hammering a dead end

MONSTERS

Lonely needs some company
To keep the monsters away
For they tend to come out of hiding
Turning the world dark and gray
Sometimes they come in the form of words
The kind that should've never been born
Those type of words would be better off dead
A death that no one would mourn
For words can cause people to break
To doubt, to lie, to cry
To make a decision; then change their minds
Or to simply say goodbye
"Sticks and stones may break my bones
But words will never hurt me"
Whoever it was that created that rhyme
I strongly disagree
Who believes monsters live in closets
Or hide beneath the bed?
I hope that you are quite aware
They live in words instead

APOLOGIES

Apologies don't mean a thing
If you don't ever try to fix it
Sometimes it's hard to find the words
Or make change such a commitment
You lie awake and wonder why
Honesty can be hard to speak
The truth can be quite painful
Staining your heart bleak
Sometimes it's easier to lie
To spare someone the pain
Guilt can leave you hollow inside
Regret's a difficult thing to explain
Time has a way of running out
On forgiveness it closes the door
For if you don't ever fix it
Sorry won't work anymore

WAR PAINT

Your life is worth the struggle
Your scars are your war paint
Don't let the monsters in your head
Plan a grand escape
You are not your demons
You are not your doubts
Remember as you hit your knees
Every prayer you whisper counts
When face to face with the devil
Do not be afraid
For the Lord is right there by your side
Leading your spiritual crusade
Don't be ashamed of who you were
Don't let your past define you
You're not the jury or the judge
Forgiveness should be pursued
Find yourself within the dark
Be stronger than your storm
With tragedy comes a second chance
For the pain to be transformed
For you are strong enough
To win the daily fight
To not give up on breathing
To focus on the light

MEMORIES

No matter how much time goes by
The memories are always there
Though they seem to be a bit faded
I can grasp them if I dare
Sleeping in footie-pajamas
Fuzzy blanket and thumb in my mouth
Afraid to get out of bed
Fearing the darkness of the house
Dreading that first day of school
Being the new kid in the class
Sensing I didn't quite fit in
Praying the day would pass
Hours spent in a studio
Dance shoes on my feet
In the front yard twirling baton
Practicing for the days I compete
Adrenaline inside the stadium
From Sunday's football crowd
Red and gold attire
The cheering echoes loud
Along came the high school years
Cheerleading and gymnastics
No confidence; low self-esteem
The bottom rung of social status
Heading off into the unknown
A sorority and dorm room
I turned 18 and knew everything
Obviously, I assumed
I liked my shots of tequila
On Thursday and Friday night
Once I had my liquid courage
Everything seemed alright
Sometimes memories are painful
They can also shine bright
Each one has created the person I am
In that I should delight

A MOTHER'S LOVE

You only have one mother
Treat her with respect
You don't want to turn around one day
To find your heart full of regret
When society knocks you down
Her love turns into wings
Lifting you far above the world
As if you were a queen or king
She has a deep devotion
She sacrifices and carries your pain
Patient and forgiving
Her love will always sustain
For all her loving kindness
She asks nothing in return
Nothing destroys her belief in you
Standing beside you at every turn
The support she offers is endless
So many ways to exhibit she cares
Selfless with her time and needs
Consistently keeping you in her prayers
Repeatedly letting you know
That to her you forever belong
No matter where life takes you
A mother's love stays strong
Never pause from learning
She has an abundance of wisdom to share
So take the time to say thank you
Make your love for her aware

Dedicated to my mom, Kathleen Petrucela
Happy 80th Birthday!

ANGEL'S WINGS

A feather is a symbol
That angels are above
It's the way that they communicate
To tell us that we're loved
So, if you find one on the ground
Make sure to whisper "thank you"
For it's a magical reminder
That they're there to help you through
Whether it's to let you know
They walk beside your struggles
Or wrap you up within their wings
To help and soothe your troubles
A feather carries hope
As it floats along the breeze
Coming to rest upon your soul
To bring your soul some ease
Don't dismiss those random feathers
Or the comfort that they bring
For they've fallen from the heavens
Straight from your angel's wings

FOOTPRINTS

The footprints that you made that day
May have washed out with the tide
The ocean's spray upon your skin
The sun rays may have dried
But the words you whispered to the waves
Crashed across the seas
Rising like a prayer to God
As they caught the ocean's breeze
Those words were meant for no one's ears
But the Lord himself
Hope, fear, pain, and joy
There was nothing you withheld
When your shoulders feel heavy
You must set your burdens free
Allowing the Lord into your heart
Is the most important key
As you walk along the sand
Give the Lord control
Watch the waves roll in and out
Let sand settle in your soul

BURNED OUT

As the day turned to night
And the sun fell asleep
A heart broke in pieces
A soul began to weep
For each tear that fell
A star flickered out
Due to unanswered prayers
The mind filled with doubt
Every door left unopened
Every candle burned down
Erased dreams of the future
And left hope to drown
When a body becomes vacant
Who's left to care
Whether a soul fights to live
Or chooses to die if it dare
Will anyone notice
One less light on this earth
As the flame smolders out
Singeing its worth

THE THREAT

The days turn into months
The months turn into years
There are times where I find myself
Thinking you should still be here
I try not to dwell
On all the moments you're missing
But then a certain song will play
Which starts me reminiscing
Of all the times we laughed
The times we may have cried
Or maybe of the times
We sat quietly side-by-side
Contemplating life
And all that it could be
Not once did it cross my mind
Tomorrow wasn't a guarantee
It's a difficult lesson that we must learn
And once learned we should never forget
Whether or not someone is dead or alive
Losing them is always a threat

A DIFFERENT LIGHT

Because your light is not like mine
And your grays fall in different shades
That doesn't mean our colors can't blend
Into perfect shining rays
Because our minds aren't always aligned
And our thoughts may disagree
Doesn't mean we can't work together
Or that success is absentee
I wish we always stayed on track
Never to stray off course
That arguments were seldom had
We never felt remorse
Relationships, no matter the type
Take work, love and care
A little take; a lot more give
Forgiveness and some prayer
That's how we blend our colors
For this great big world to see
Accepting each other's differences
Is a very important key

BYSTANDER

Why can't I be forgiven
For mistakes from my past?
Are you going to hold a grudge
That my life cannot outlast?
I sit and cry an ocean
Not knowing what to think
The knowledge that my guts you hate
Leaves me holding my breath
Praying to sink
I've never been so broken
As I am right now
For to you I am invisible
No relationship allowed
I can't go back and change the way
Things were said and done
Words were spilled with anger
Remember, mine weren't the only ones
 I can't let the past pollute my heart
With bitterness, distrust, and anger
I will continue to work on forgiving you
It's your choice to remain a bystander

THE DISAPPEARANCE

She walked right out the front door
Straight into the night
Swallowed up in darkness
She disappeared from sight
No trace of where she might have gone
Just trees whispering her name
The moon stays hidden behind clouds
Afraid it might be blamed
The night creatures keep her secret
As they themselves creep through the trees
Not even the stars above
Can safely guarantee
That when the moon and sun
Switch places in the sky
That she'll walk back through the front door
And to the darkness say goodbye

ROAD MAP

Feeling like you're stuck
Living a life that's extra boring
All the world is traveling
Weekends spent exploring
You see it in all the pictures
On those social media posts
Filtered to perfection
Labeled with creative quotes
But is anyone truly where
They think they want to be?
Always chasing the next best thing
In search of their destiny
The grass isn't always greener
On the other side of the fence
Life isn't something that you win
It's a series of events
Moments full of chaos
Heartache and mistakes
Grace and second chances
Memories to embrace
Stop trying to fit in
Chasing a dream that isn't yours
For within life's messiness
Is your very own path to explore
Step beyond the filters
Make peace with all your flaws
Life isn't a race to the finish
It's okay to stop and pause
Find out what is important
Along the road map you call life
Kindness, people, love
Always keeping faith in sight

BROKEN AND WHOLE

I swear that I'm not crazy
Maybe just a little impaired
I know you can't tell who I am anymore
I know that you don't really care
You remember how I used to be
Blind to the load that I carry
Dragging around what brings me down
My problems I try to bury
I find friends within the shadows
They embrace my broken pieces
Having trouble knowing my place in this world
I release my pain to Jesus
All of us are both broken and whole
Each with journeys to embark
As you look at yourself in the mirror
Remember we're all the same in the dark

CLEANSING

When the rainy days dry up
And I begin to feel parched
I ride the ocean waves
Until my heartbeat is recharged
Listening to its rhythm
'Til once again, my eyes shed tears
The waterfall is cleansing
As my soul's graffiti starts to clear
Every breath of air
Is like inhaling memories
The Lord knows what it is I've lost
And how my heart's in jeopardy
I'm afraid to turn around
I may see part of myself die
I can't change where I've been
The past can't be denied
I've lived, I've learned
I've drowned, I've burned
To be understood
Is what I yearn
I want to bottle up
Those crashing ocean waves
To cleanse me from nights that never end
To save me from a shallow grave

IN THE CORNER OF MY MIND

In the corner of my mind
The shadows creep and crawl
Tucked inside those cobwebs
A dark side awaits its call
I do my best to keep it
Under lock and key
For if it sees the light of day
The good vibes try to flee
What lurks within the shadows
Is a very wicked being
Compiled of closet skeletons
And a "what if" type of grieving
If it sneaks across the line
To slither out and play
My words will sound like begging
As I kneel down to pray

ARTWORK OF LIFE

There are times we all screw up
Days where jealousy takes control
We are all human beings filled with errors
With a series of incidents and regrets
Should we define each other by any one single choice?
We are all sinner and saint
In need of grace and forgiveness
Life is an infinite game
We may not always understand what is happening
Until the end of one season and the beginning of another
It takes mistakes, failures, and successes
To create our own artwork of life
Sometimes we battle the devil
Sometimes the devil wins
But even though there are times
That God gives us more than we can handle
God shows us He can make something beautiful
Out of all our broken pieces

WRITER'S BLOCK

I kind of want to sit and write
So far nothing comes to mind
The pencil sits upon the paper
But words I cannot find
My mind is constantly overflowing
Yet my thoughts are running blank
As if all the words have gone and drowned
Within my own thinking tank
I just want to pen my ramblings
Clogging up my brain
Letting them flow freely
Like a storm cloud releasing rain
Instead, they remain all jumbled up
Stacking a mile high
All that remains for me to do
Is to release a heavy sigh

I WISH I WAS LIKE CINDERELLA

I wish I was like Cinderella
Sadly, I am not
Instead, I'm like her stepsisters
Who the prince has never sought
My life is not a fairy tale
On my head there sits no crown
I dress in jeans and old t-shirts
Not a beautiful sparkly gown
There are no servants to wait on me
Just my own two hands and feet
No knight in shining armor
Making loneliness obsolete
I've learned to fight the battles
Of rejection and heartache
To look at fear straight in the eye
Admit to my mistakes
I'm thankful for my imagination
Courage and self-esteem
Allowing for opportunity
To live in my own dream

Inspired by the novel
Stepsister by Jennifer Donnelly

THIEF

Bubbling just below the surface
Murkiness muddles clarity
Tears threaten to spill over
With somewhat regularity
The dam tends to break
During the witching hour
When the house is sound asleep
Despair an unwanted prowler
Confused about the sadness
Hidden beneath the skin
Robbing all joy and laughter
Shoving thoughts into a tailspin
It's as if the clock is broken
And time is standing still
Nothing seems to fix it
Not even a prescribed pill
As dawn begins its slow approach
Teardrops leave their stain
Each remaining mark
A memory of the pain

HE COLLECTS MY PIECES

He collects my pieces
As I crack and break
He never looks at me
As if I was a mistake
He never walks away
Or brings up the past
Never does He treat me
Like a misfit or outcast
Constant and steady
Continuously at my side
No matter my mistakes
His love is not denied
He collects my tears
Rejoices with my smile
And when my world is upside down
He reminds me life's worthwhile
He helps me find strength
To pray more than worry
Leading me towards
Finding joy in my journey

DIFFERENT SHORES

We live on different lands
An ocean's width away
As your day is just beginning
My moon comes out to play
I may not be able to hold your hand
Or lay down by your side
But my heart still beats with thoughts of you
No matter how wide the divide
This journey may not be an easy one
Yet it's the path our souls did choose
Some people may not understand
But their feet aren't in our shoes
Whispered secrets through the phone
Desires for our future
Constantly battling the thousands of miles
Separating us like an intruder
We send our prayers across the waves
Where hope and fear collide
Wondering how long until news is heard
On when we can reunite
Until then, we must remain
Standing on distant shores
As our prayers caress the sand
Remember…
You are mine and I am yours

Dedicated to James O'Brien and Natnicha Plengpradab
September 2021

WHISPERED WISHES

A whisper floats along the breeze
Spreading across the land
It carries someone's hopes and dreams
Released from the palm of their hand
Wishes made on a dandelion
Or clover with four leaves
Attaching to the wing of a dragonfly
Resting on a sunbeam
Warmth feeds those hopes and dreams
Until they begin to bloom
Scattering wishes far and wide
Releasing butterflies from their cocoon

CONFINED

Gazing out the window
The world seems far away
Trapped inside of the unknown
Satan begins to play
Creeping through the playground
Its sandbox filled with doubt
Depression swinging back and forth
Anxiety begins to mount
Walking down the hallway
A million questions on the mind
Wondering how much longer
This world will stay confined
Locked in isolation
As hope begins to dim
Fighting a spiritual warfare
Whispering prayers from deep within
Praying for the world to heal
Activities to be revived
To once again walk the outdoors
With a spiritual faith that survived

Pandemic Lockdown 2020

SO MANY BROKEN PIECES

So many broken pieces
So many crumbling walls
Too many cracks to trip on
Creating far too many falls
I am barely breathing
I am falling apart
Mountains of doubt inside my head
Plenty of pain to pierce my heart
Brokenness is all around
Found in darkness and in light
Masked by the smile on my face
My tattered pieces continue to fight
Trying to find meaning within the broken
Healing light becomes a bandage
Finally helping me to see
That I am beautifully damaged

ROOT OF EVIL

Where everyone claims
That they're not at fault
Everyone else is to blame
It is easier to judge
And to criticize
Then to look in the mirror
At their own demise
They'd rather hurt others
And generate pain
Actions and words
Cause society to complain
Too much hatred
And non acceptance
Is the root of evil
Spreading our world with vengeance

TIRED EYES

Just want to give up on trying
To find the right words to say
Worn out by conversations
People who never stay
Some have good intentions
Yet don't fully understand
What it may feel like
To hold an empty hand
Just want to stop fighting
Just want to let go
Release all the burdens
That perpetually overflow
Feet that keep on sinking
Tired eyes that get no rest
Constantly failing
Life's little test
You don't know what it's like
To live in these shoes
As you look into my eyes
Try to find some clues
Please don't tell me what you see
Or all that my eyes betray
For once I want to just let go
Admit I'm not okay

THE PAST

Defeated by the troubles
That you can't seem to repair
Stumbling around in life
Drowning in despair
Searching through your playlist
For that perfectly sad song
Hoping that rhythm and words
Are enough to keep you strong
Can you find it in your heart
To mend transgressions made?
By others and by your own self
Putting forgiveness on display
You can't keep carrying your haunted past
With you towards the future
It will steal your finest treasures
Just like a masked intruder

SCARS

I walk hand in hand with uncertainty
Miles upon miles each day
Trying to decide which path to take
As I confessed to the Lord today
My heart tugs me in one direction
My mind signals a different route
Leaving my soul conflicted
Causing temptation to lash out
Some say happiness will find me
But I've learned that sadness will too
It sneaks right up behind me
Just when I thought I'd make it through
Sadness is that feeling
When falling doesn't stop
It steals life of meaning
Blinding me from all I've got
I can't remember how it started
I don't know when it'll come to an end
Nothing seems to make sense
Until it does, I will just pretend
My body reveals its history
With an endless amount of scars
Invisible tokens of joy and sorrow
Too many to count, just like the stars
The ugliest ones I try burying
But the wounds continually persist
Their pain a consistent reminder
That my scars will forever exist
I refuse to be ashamed
Of those scars living in my skin
For they carry truth and proof
That with God by my side I will win

BOOKWORM

If I could live inside a book
Which character would I be?
Maybe a damsel in distress
Or a mermaid in the sea?
I could choose to be a hero
Or the detective fighting crime
The subject of an author's poem
Or a witch with a spell to rhyme
I could lose myself within the plot
Page one straight through the end
Only to place it back on the shelf
Choose another and begin again
Find myself lost in adventure
Fairy tale, mystery, or war
My favorite place to disappear
Is in the aisles of a bookstore

COUNTRY LIVING

Gazing across the valley
Farmland everywhere
Hay bales dot the fields
Smell of mint lingers in the air
Several combines hum
From one of the distant farms
It's a sound that I think
Holds some country charm
The screech of a hawk
As it flies overhead
Out on a hunt
With wings widespread
A light summer breeze
Rustles through the oak tree
The red, white, and blue
Waves its freedom at me
No shoes on my feet
As I rest on my deck
Gazing across the valley
With a continuing respect

HALO AND HORNS

In my closet hangs a halo
Right next to a pair of horns
Some days my personality
Takes on different forms
I try to wear a smile
Spread kindness where I can
But the devil sometimes sneaks right in
And messes with that plan
My goal is positivity
To have a glass half full
Sporadically the negative
Replaces it with bull
I try to fight the sarcasm
The judgment and critique
I know that words can burn and scar
If not careful what I speak
Since I'm only human
 I tend to make mistakes
Apologies roll off my tongue
I often fall from grace
I learn from every stumble
Each mountain that I climb
Staying focused on the heavens
Seeking strength from the divine

SUMMER'S TREASURE

I'm a fan of summer
Cool creeks, tan legs and beer
Country music festivals
And spotted baby deer
Long days filled with sunshine
Red tail hawks that own the sky
A feeling of contentment
The awe of a dragonfly
Yummy deep pit barbeques
With family, who I also call friends
A weekend spent with cousins
Which is something I must recommend
Daily evening walks
My best friend by my side
A pile of new books to read
Hours of entertainment they provide
My heart and soul would be satisfied
If summer could last forever
For once the sky starts releasing tears
It will drown out my summer's treasure

Reasons

When all is said and done
And my time ceases to exist
I hope that I have left behind
Reasons to be missed
I definitely haven't been perfect
But then again, neither have you
That's part of being human
In the end, we all pay our dues
There are times I have been hurt
Others where I've caused the pain
There've been many things I've said and done
That I just can't seem to explain
I think it would be easier
If we lived life in reverse
We'd carry deeper wisdom
From death until our birth
Maybe make fewer mistakes
Suffer a few less broken hearts
Discover how to make a difference
Before this life we must depart
Take time to do something that matters
Touch some hearts along the way
Say something that has meaning
Don't let the devil lead you astray

SKELETONS

Everyone has skeletons
Hanging in their closet
Tucked into the shadows
Where no one else can see
For mistakes are represented
By bones put on display
Then buried beneath the surface
Where hopefully they will stay
Beware of digging up
Someone else's carnage
For nothing will grow from tainted dirt
And your shovel will end up tarnished

HER CREATION

She travels through the universe
Skipping across the stars
Placing them upon her heart
Including the ones with scars
Some continue burning bright
Over months and years
Others tend to dim and fall
Leaving her shedding tears
Some are stored away
Where their memories burn
Others fizzle out and die
Leaving her heart to yearn
Every star that she collects
Adds to her creation
Fashioning her into who she'll be
For the rest of her life's duration

LOVE HAS A NAME

Jesus knows our hardships
Our losses, our regret
The things we've never told
The things we try to forget
We each have a longing inside
A yearning to be known
Desire for people to know our name
For acceptance and love to be shown
For love stands by someone
When there's no one else who will
We shouldn't be defined by our mistakes
Ask forgiveness, pray and be still
We tend to place labels on people
On this, we must improve
Love has a name; it's called Jesus
He offers us grace and truth

REGRET'S TATTOO

The mind's wall is beat up
As anxiety and worry tumble about
Like waves crashing upon the ocean's shoreline
Shattering confidence into fragments
Leaving it scattered around
Unable to piece it back together
Second guessing decisions
Reflecting on life choices
From the outside looking in
It's hard to understand
Peering out from inside the mind
It's hard to explain
So much self-doubt rushes in
Washing away faith's footprints
Leaving a blank surface
For regret's tattoo

A HANDBOOK

I wish that life was simpler
With a handbook full of plans
One filled with directions
For all of life's demands
To guide through times of trouble
Offer advice when moods are low
Step by step solutions
To problems as they grow
Maybe I'd fail less often
Make fewer dumb mistakes
Keep myself from stumbling
Avoid moments of disgrace
Save myself from heartache
Disappointment that drowns the soul
A handbook might protect me
From a life out of control

I'M FINE

I need the pain to be gone
It hurts so bad I can't breathe
The fist of anxiety
Continuously chokes me
It's like I'm screaming
Yet no one can hear
As one by one my dreams die
And all hope disappears
The flames of panic
Are all consuming
The mind is corrupted
With negativity pursuing
I don't receive a response
When I cry out for God
Could the reason be
That I'm mentally flawed?
I walk amongst millions
Who experience my pain
Invisible to each other
Due to the "I'm Fine" campaign

RAISE MY VOICE AND PRAY

When I turn on the tv
And all the news is bad
God is taken out of schools
They've stopped standing for our flag
When I'm losing my direction
And my feet can't find their way
A million unanswered questions
Satan leads the world astray
Everyone is so divided
Quick to take offense
My faith can feel shaken
When things aren't making sense
There's a lot that I don't understand
Even more I can't control
I turn to the one that'll save me
Let a calm settle in my soul
It's the only thing that'll get me through
Find some good in every day
Just talk like I'm talking to a friend
Raise my voice and pray

PLAYLIST

When my thoughts are heavy
Worry weighing on my mind
I drown myself in music
Disappearing for a time
Let a song tug a memory
From another time
Another place
Scroll through my playlist
Until I hear lyrics that relate
Crank up the volume
Block out the world around
Lose myself within my headphones
Melody the only sound

HOMEWARD BOUND

I can't blame you for leaving
But it's still not fair
I hope where you have gone
To someday meet you there
If I had known the last time
Would have been the last
I'd have stayed a little longer
 Shared a few more laughs
The road you walked wasn't easy
You collected scars along the way
I've talked to God about you
He's promised me you're now okay
That doesn't keep the tears from falling
Like an ocean from my eyes
Whenever my gaze turns upward
Toward the Heaven in the sky
At times I don't know what to do
Now that you're not here
I'm afraid your voice and image
Will slowly disappear
Send me a sign to remember
All that's good and true
To keep me on the road
That will bring me home to you

YOU AND I

You and I have been side by side
For more than half our lives
It's been a long and windy road
Mixed with both sunny and stormy skies
We each have made countless mistakes
Ranging from big to small
What I love about the two of us
Is we're in it for the long haul
I admire your desire for helping out others
And how you make friends wherever we go
You have a passion for the great outdoors
And you're not too old to play legos
I'm thankful for all the times
You stood right by my side
Even when life felt
Like we were caught in a riptide
Thank you for forgiving
Every bad decision I've made
Walking with you through this thing called life
Is not something I'm willing to trade

Happy 28th Anniversary to my husband!
02/12/2022

ABOUT THE AUTHOR

Kathryn M. Boyd lives in the Pacific Northwest with her husband, Charles, and is a mother of three adult children. She has been writing poetry for 37 years and has been a published poet since 2018. Kathryn has a passion for books and for writing. She has always found penning her thoughts and prayers onto paper gives her the creative outlet needed for her poetry.

PREVIOUS WORKS

Poetry Soup

Kathryn M. Boyd

Poetry Soup - Poems are for all who acknowledge the messy, imperfect, and real side of themselves. Never surrender.

https://www.amazon.com/Poetry-Soup-Kathryn-M-Boyd/dp/1986679152

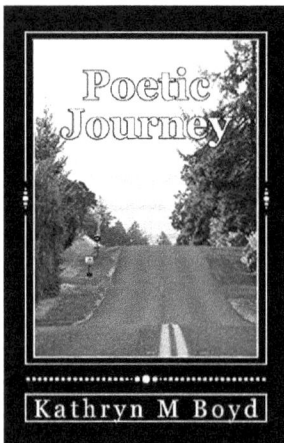

Poetic Journey - A collection of poetry about life's journey; the hardships, the blessings, inner demons, and guardian angels.

https://www.amazon.com/Poetic-Journey-Kathryn-M-Boyd/dp/1727516478

www.ingramcontent.com/pod-product-compliance
Lightning Source LLC
Chambersburg PA
CBHW071836020426
42331CB00007B/1744